Make Me Giggle

WRITING YOUR OWN SILLY STORY

by Nancy Loewen

illustrated by Cori Doerrfeld

Picture Window Books
Minneapolis, Minnesota

Editor: Jill Kalz
Designer: Nathan Gassman
Page Production: Melissa Kes
Editorial Director: Nick Healy
Creative Director: Joe Ewest
The illustrations in this book were created with acrylics.

Picture Window Books
1710 Roe Crest Drive
North Mankato, MN 56003
www.capstonepub.com

Library of Congress Cataloging-in-Publication Data
Loewen, Nancy, 1964–
Make me giggle : writing your own silly story /
by Nancy Loewen ; illustrated by Cori Doerrfeld.
p. cm. — (Writer's toolbox)
Includes index.
ISBN 978-1-4048-5518-2 (library binding)
ISBN 978-1-4048-5704-9 (paperback)
1. Child authors—Handbooks, manuals, etc.—
Juvenile literature. 2. Humorous stories—Authorship—
Juvenile literature. 3. Creative writing—Juvenile literature.
I. Doerrfeld, Cori, ill. II. Title.
PN171.C5L64 2009
808'.0683—dc22   2009003297

Printed in the United States of America in North Mankato, Minnesota.
022013   007196R

Special thanks to our adviser,
Terry Flaherty, Ph.D., Professor of English,
Minnesota State University, Mankato,
for his expertise.

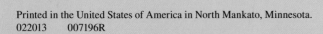

Feeling hungry? Today's special is a silly story sundae. This yummy treat has two scoops of smiles and one scoop of tee-hee. It's smothered in whipped laughter and sprinkled with giggles!

Silly stories make us laugh. They stretch our imaginations. They let us take a break from the serious things in our lives.

Read the following story, *The Problem Purr*. Then go back to page 5 and start learning about the tools you need to write your own silly story.

Fritter looked like an ordinary kitten. He had two pointed ears. He had a pink nose and an even pinker tongue. He had whiskers, sharp little claws, and a long curvy tail.

But Fritter was not an ordinary kitten.

When Fritter purred, mice scampered into their holes. Dogs whined. Frogs dove into deep water, and rabbits tied their ears into knots.

~ Tool 1 ~

The beginning of a silly story should introduce one or more main **CHARACTERS**. Characters are the people, animals, or creatures in a story. Main characters are the ones who appear most often. Here we learn a lot about Fritter the kitten. Fritter is one of the story's main characters.

~ Tool 2 ~

The **SETTING** is the time and place in which a story happens. We see from the illustrations here that this story takes place on a farm. And, like many silly stories, it happens in its own time—set apart from real life.

Fritter's purr sounded a bit like a lawn mower sputtering ... a hippopotamus hiccupping ... a goose honking. It reminded some folks of a squeaky barn door or the braying of a hopping-mad donkey.

Fritter's purr sounded something like this:

putt-putt-hic-HONK-squeak-HEE-HAW!

And it was LOUD!

~ Tool 3 ~

Silly stories are filled with **SILLINESS**: silly characters, places, names, events, and sounds. Things don't have to make sense, and they're not likely to happen in real life. For example, have you ever heard a *real* kitten make such a silly sound?

~ Tool 4 ~

IMAGERY can be a big part of silly stories. Writers use words to create a picture in readers' minds. The words might compare one thing to another. Here Fritter's purr is compared to a lawn mower, a hiccupping hippo, a goose, a squeaky barn door, and a mad donkey.

His mother tried to train Fritter to purr properly.

~ Tool 5 ~

WORD SOUNDS can make a silly story more fun. Rhyming words—such as *rumble tumble fumble bumble*—create a pleasing sound. Repeating consonant sounds also get the reader's attention. In the first sentence on this page, for example, notice the many r's, t's, and p's.

"Breathe slow and steady," she said. "Think *rumble tumble fumble bumble* as you picture dancing spots of light. That always works for me when my purr gets stuck."

So Fritter closed his eyes. He breathed slowly and steadily. He thought *rumble tumble fumble bumble*. He pictured dancing spots of light. But out came ...

putt-putt-hic-HONK-squeak-HEE-HAW!

His father, too, tried to train Fritter to purr properly.

"Imagine there's a tiny motor inside of you. Turn the key. Shift into gear. Now slowly give your little motor the gas."

Fritter closed his eyes and pictured everything his father had described.

Out came ...
putt-putt-hic-
HONK-squeak-
HEE-HAW!

"Slam on the brakes!"
his father shouted.

Fritter's brothers and sisters tried something different.

"I've got your tail!"

~ Tool 6 ~

DIALOGUE is what characters say to each other. Through dialogue, readers learn about the characters and get information about the story's events. Dialogue makes readers feel like they're *hearing* a story, not just reading it.

"Bet you can't catch me!"

"I dare you to climb to the top of the light pole!"

"I double-dare you to go into the doghouse!"

They kept Fritter so busy that he didn't have time to purr.

If Fritter did have a quiet, peaceful moment, the other barnyard animals were quick to put gloomy thoughts into his head.

"Cold wind," said the horse.

"An empty food dish," said the dog.

"Three straight days of rain," said the sheep.

"Thanksgiving," said the turkey.

But Fritter was a cheerful kitten, and he could hold his purrs inside for only so long. At some point, he had to let go.

putt-putt-hic-HONK-squeak-HEE-HAW!

~ Tool 7 ~

IRONY is a kind of humor. It's based on the opposite meanings of words or ideas. We would never expect anyone to try to make a friend unhappy. But in this silly story it's understandable. And for most of us, Thanksgiving is a happy thought—but not for the turkey who's dinner!

After one especially loud outburst, Madam Gallup stomped her hoof. "Fritter, you have to do something about that purr," she said. "The dog is nearly deaf. The chickens' eggs are cracking. And the mice have all moved to the next county. If you can't manage that purr of yours, I'm afraid you'll need to find another place to live."

Fritter's purr left him as quickly as it had started. He didn't have the slightest bit of a purr inside him now. Not even a single *putt*. Not even the tiniest squeak.

~ Tool 8 ~

EXAGGERATION is a great tool in writing silly stories. When writers exaggerate, they make things sound bigger or better (or smaller or worse) than they actually are. Ordinary things go over-the-top. In silly stories, it's okay to stretch the truth!

17

That night, Fritter hardly slept. He was too worried. He loved his home and didn't want to leave.

~ Tool 9 ~

The things that happen in a story are the **PLOT**. The events are connected. One thing leads to another. Each of Fritter's silly purrs has led us to this worrisome moment.

He was still awake when old Mr. Freckles shuffled to the top of the barn. The rooster ruffled his graying feathers. He opened his beak. "Cockadoodledoo," he croaked. "Cockadoodledoo."

But the barnyard stayed quiet. No one stirred.

Mr. Freckles tried again. "Ahem." He took a deep breath. "Cockadoodledoo."

Nothing.

Fritter climbed up the silo and leaped onto the roof.

Mr. Freckles blinked at him. "Why, Fritter," he said. "Thank goodness you're here. I can't seem to muster up a proper cockadoodledoo. I'm getting too old for this job."

"Let me help," Fritter said.

He gazed at the sliver of sun rising over the horizon. He looked at the lilacs, the light pole, and the doghouse. He breathed in the fresh, dewy air. He simply allowed his happiness to grow inside him, until out came the loudest, most shocking purr Fritter had ever purred.

putt putt hic HONK squeak hee HAW!

~ Tool 10 ~

Some silly stories have a bit of **SUSPENSE**. We aren't sure what's going to happen to Fritter now. We feel uncertain and worried, but a little excited, too.

Sleepy animals stumbled into the yard. They all stared up at Fritter and Mr. Freckles.

Fritter stopped purring and began to tremble. Was he in even more trouble now?

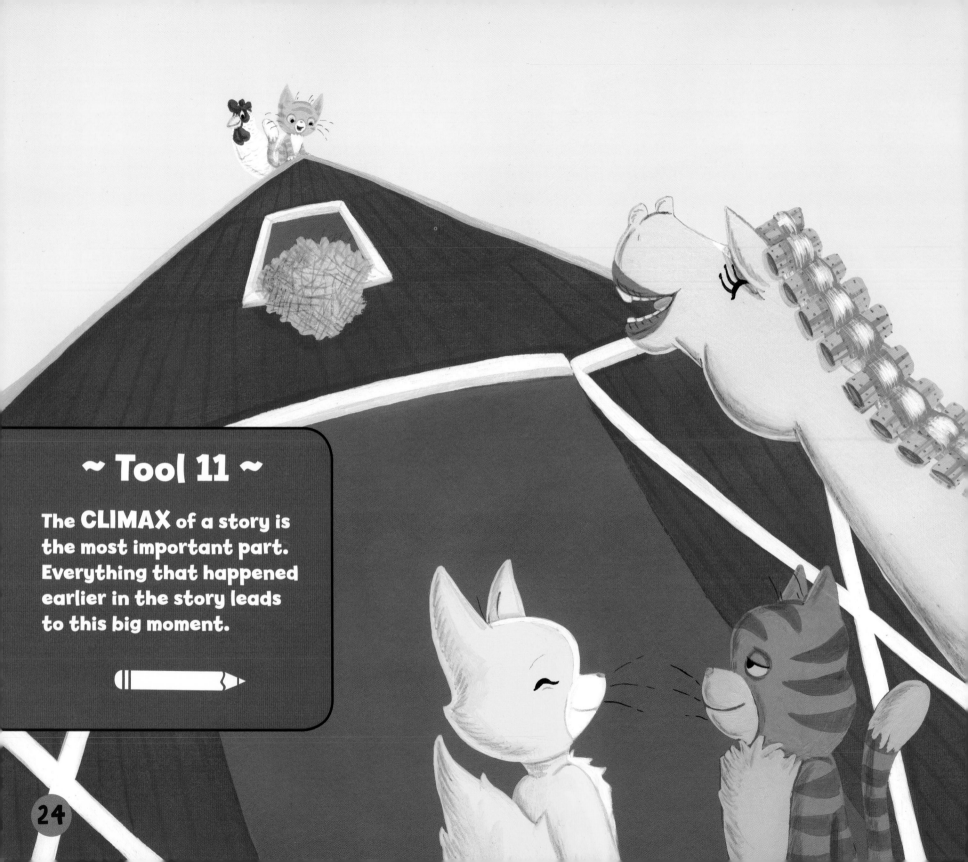

~ Tool 11 ~

The **CLIMAX** of a story is the most important part. Everything that happened earlier in the story leads to this big moment.

24

Madame Gallup huddled with Fritter's parents. They whispered and nodded. Then Madame Gallup called up to him.

"Fritter, do you think you could save up your purrs all day and night, and then give us one big wake-up purr every morning?"

Fritter could hardly believe his ears. "Yes, ma'am!" he replied. "I think I could!"

"Then that will be your new job. A predictable purr is something we can all learn to live with. Congratulations!" Madam Gallup said.

"As for you, Mr. Freckles," Madame Gallup added with a bow, "the barnyard thanks you for your years of loyal service."

Mr. Freckles' eyes grew big. "You mean, I can retire?"

"Absolutely," Madame Gallup said.

"Woo hoo!" Mr. Freckles cried. "Pack your bags, Mrs. Freckles! We're taking that trip to Florida!"

Fritter couldn't help purring some more. But no one minded. The animals were all making a lot of noise themselves—cheering.

~ Tool 12 ~

EMOTIONS play a part in all stories, even silly ones. We wouldn't feel nearly as happy for Fritter here if Mr. Freckles didn't want to retire. But since he's thrilled, we can enjoy the moment.

~ Tool 13 ~

In the **ENDING** of a silly story, all the loose ends are tied up. The reader feels happy and satisfied.

Let's Review!

These are the **13 tools** you need to write great silly stories.

The beginning of a silly story introduces the main **CHARACTERS (1)** and the **SETTING (2)**. **SILLINESS (3)** can appear in all sorts of ways—characters, places, names, and so on. Using **IMAGERY (4)** and funny **WORD SOUNDS (5)** can make a silly story even sillier.

Characters talk to each other through **DIALOGUE (6)**. **IRONY (7)** is a way of linking the opposite meanings of words or ideas. **EXAGGERATION (8)** stretches reality and adds to the fun.

One event leads to another in a story's **PLOT (9)**. A silly story might contain **SUSPENSE (10)**. In a story's **CLIMAX (11)**, the plot reaches a peak, and the major problem of the story is solved. Showing the **EMOTIONS (12)** of the characters gets the reader more involved in the story. The **ENDING (13)** should leave the reader feeling satisfied.

Getting Started Exercises

- Think about some of your favorite riddles and jokes. Could you build a story around any of them? For example, you've probably heard the joke, "Why did the chicken cross the road? To get to the other side!" Figure out your own answer to that question. What if the chicken crossed the road to meet her long-lost love, the fox? What if the chicken crossed the road to get away from her pesky little chicks?

- If you have the chance to be around toddlers or preschoolers, listen to what they say. They are just learning how to talk and put their ideas together, and their mistakes can be very funny! Maybe you'll get a story idea from them.

- Keep your own laughter journal. Carry a small notebook and record all the things that make you laugh. After a day or two, you'll probably have plenty of ideas.

- Create a group silly story. Pass a notebook around, with everyone adding one or two silly sentences. You'll have a silly story in no time!

Writing Tips

If you want to write in rhyme, use a rhyming dictionary. (You can find one at the library or on the Internet.) Seeing a list of rhyming words can spark your imagination. In silly stories, it's OK to make up words, too!

Writing a silly story can be hard work. You probably won't get your story just right on the first try. Keep working at it until you're happy. Revision is a big part of the writing process.

"Point of view" is a writing term for who is telling the story. *The Problem Purr* is told in the third person. That means a narrator tells the story using names or pronouns such as "he" or "she." "Albert ate 101 grapes" and "He ate 101 grapes" are examples of third-person point of view. In the first-person point of view, "I" tells the story. "I ate 101 grapes" is an example of first-person point of view. Stories can be told either way. Try both, and see which is funnier for your story.

Glossary

characters—the people, animals, or creatures in a story

climax—a story's most exciting moment

compare—to liken one thing to another

consonant—a letter of the alphabet other than *a*, *e*, *i*, *o*, and *u*

dialogue—the words spoken between two or more characters; in writing, dialogue is set off with quotation marks

emotions—feelings

ending—the story's finish

events—things that happen

exaggeration—overstating, going beyond the truth

illustrations—artwork that shows scenes from a story

imagery—words used to create pictures in readers' minds

irony—a kind of humor based on the opposite meanings of words or ideas

plot—what happens in a story

predictable—turning out in a way that was expected

repeating—doing, saying, or making something again and again

retire—to take oneself away from a job

revision—a change, a "re-vision" of something, seeing it in a new way

rhyming—words that end with the same sounds, such as *cat* and *rat*

setting—the time and place of a story

suspense—worry, unease

To Learn More

More Books to Read

Barrett, Judi. *Cloudy with a Chance of Meatballs.* New York: Aladdin Books, 1982.

Bartram, Simon. *Man on the Moon: A Day in the Life of Bob.* Cambridge, Mass.: Candlewick Press, 2002.

Briggs, Raymond. *Ug: Boy Genius of the Stone Age.* New York: Alfred A. Knopf, 2002.

Cronin, Doreen, and Betsy Lewin. *Thump, Quack, Moo: A Whacky Adventure.* New York: Atheneum Books for Young Readers, 2008.

Internet Sites

FactHound offers a safe, fun way to find Internet sites related to this book. All of the sites on FactHound have been researched by our staff.

Here's all you do:
Visit *www.facthound.com*
FactHound will fetch the best sites for you!

Index

Look for all of the books in the Writer's Toolbox series:

It's All About You: Writing Your Own Journal
Just the Facts: Writing Your Own Research Report
Make Me Giggle: Writing Your Own Silly Story
Once Upon a Time: Writing Your Own Fairy Tale

Share a Scare: Writing Your Own Scary Story
Show Me a Story: Writing Your Own Picture Book
Sincerely Yours: Writing Your Own Letter
Words, Wit, and Wonder: Writing Your Own Poem